GRAPHIC HEROES OF THE AMERICAN REVOLUTION

THOMAS PAINE WRITES
COMMON SENSE

BY GARY JEFFREY
ILLUSTRATED BY NICK SPENDER

Gareth Stevens
Publishing

Please visit our website, www.garethstevens.com.
For a free color catalog of all our high-quality books,
call toll free 1-800-542-2595 or fax 1-877-542-2596.

Library of Congress Cataloging-in-Publication Data

Jeffrey, Gary.
Thomas Paine writes Common Sense / Gary Jeffrey.
p. cm. — (Graphic heroes of the American Revolution)
Includes index.
ISBN 978-1-4339-6029-1 (pbk.)
ISBN 978-1-4339-6030-7 (6-pack)
ISBN 978-1-4339-6028-4 (library binding)
1. Paine, Thomas, 1737-1809—Juvenile literature. 2. Paine, Thomas,
1737-1809. Common sense—Juvenile literature. 3. United States—Politics
and government--1775-1783—Juvenile literature. I. Title.
JC178.V2J44 2011
320.01'1—dc22

2011000888

First Edition

Published in 2012 by
Gareth Stevens Publishing
111 East 14th Street, Suite 349
New York, NY 10003

Copyright © 2012 David West Books

Designed by David West Books
Editor: Ronne Randall

Photo credits:
p5, Library of Congress; p22, austinevan

Printed in China

CPSIA compliance information: Batch #DS11GS: For further information contact Gareth Stevens, New York, New York at 1-800-542-2595.

CONTENTS

In 1775 they stood armed and ready, but among the patriots, there were still arguments about how far they should go in their fight with the British. Some wanted to stay loyal to the king while fighting for fair treatment. Others called for outright independence—a new country of their own.

The Boston Tea Party in 1773 had shown the patriots' resolve.

A REVOLUTIONARY IDEA

The idea of separating from Britain had been floated since the troubles began. Many rich Americans shuddered at the thought of such extreme action. Ordinary Americans were largely unaware. The arguments in favor had been put in such high-flown language that they were shut out. Independence was a cause championed by the patriot elite.

Thomas Jefferson had promoted the idea of independence in 1774.

A NE'ER-DO-WELL

Thomas Paine was born in Norfolk in the east of England. His father was a corset maker, and Paine's first job was as his apprentice. Fed up with stay making, he tried his hand at being a sailor, a schoolteacher, and a shopkeeper, but none of them took.

Finally, he became a tax collector but got fired when he wrote a rabble-rousing pamphlet that demanded better pay. In London, he met Benjamin Franklin, who advised him to try his luck in America and gave him a letter of introduction.

Paine was thirty-eight when he landed in America as a penniless ne'er-do-well.

The capital, Philadelphia, was the intellectual and commercial heart of the colonies.

NEW WORLD—NEW START

Franklin's letter got Paine a position writing and editing a new magazine in Philadelphia—a job he could do brilliantly.

Paine watched with interest the strife-torn events that were unfolding around him, all the while hoping that a peaceful solution could still be found…

Thomas Paine Writes
COMMON SENSE

THE OFFICES OF THE PENNSYLVANIA MAGAZINE, PHILADELPHIA, APRIL 20, 1775.

IT'S WAR!

THOMAS PAINE HAD JUST BEEN PUTTING THE FINISHING TOUCHES ON AN ARTICLE ABOUT **SLAVERY** WHEN **BENJAMIN FRANKLIN** HAD BURST IN.

PAINE CONTINUED WORKING AT THE MAGAZINE, WRITING PIECES SUPPORTING THE REBELS.

I KNOW HOW IT FEELS TO BE UNDER THE **HEEL** OF THE ESTABLISHMENT.

IN BRITAIN, HE HAD COME UNDER FIRE FOR STANDING UP FOR PEOPLE'S RIGHTS.

PAINE WATCHED FROM THE SIDELINES AS A NEW CONTINENTAL ARMY, LED BY GEORGE WASHINGTON, BESIEGED THE BRITISH IN BOSTON AND FOUGHT A FEROCIOUS BATTLE AT BUNKER HILL.

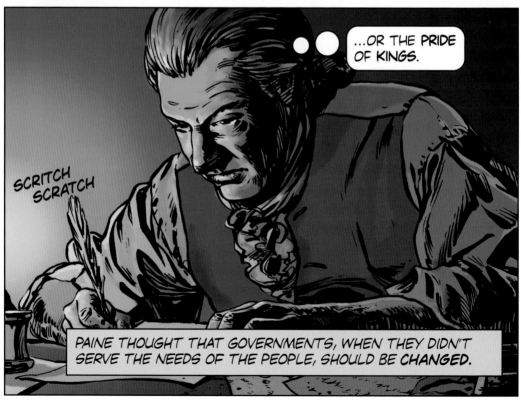

HOWEVER, NOT ALL PATRIOTS AGREED WITH EVERYTHING IN THE PAMPHLET.

HIS IDEAS ABOUT GOVERNMENT ARE *TOO* REVOLUTIONARY!

– JUST A RECIPE FOR A *DIFFERENT* KIND OF TYRANNY!

JOHN ADAMS KNEW THAT A LASTING DEMOCRACY NEEDED RESPONSIBLE POLITICIANS, RATHER THAN A MOB, TO LEAD IT.

WHATEVER ITS SHORTCOMINGS, "COMMON SENSE" HAD SET PUBLIC OPINION FIRMLY BEHIND A DECLARATION OF INDEPENDENCE.

AN IDEA THAT HAD BEEN *UNTHINKABLE* TO MANY THE YEAR BEFORE.

THE END

"These are the times that try men's souls..." wrote Thomas Paine in the winter of 1776. The rebels had lost New York, and all was gloom. Washington had the first of Paine's "American Crisis" pamphlets read out to his troops before the Battle of Trenton. Paine's words inspired them to an important victory. Paine served as a soldier and a diplomat during the war. In the 1783 victory parade in Philadelphia, he rode alongside George Washington.

Paine encouraged the army in the early years with a series of pamphlets entitled "The American Crisis."

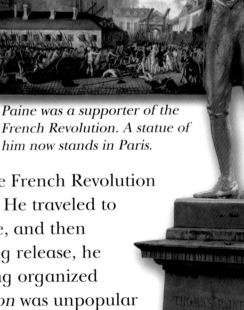

Paine was a supporter of the French Revolution. A statue of him now stands in Paris.

REVOLUTION BOOSTER

In 1791, Paine wrote a pamphlet in support of the French Revolution called *The Rights of Man*. He traveled to France, was honored there, and then imprisoned! While awaiting release, he wrote a pamphlet attacking organized religion. *The Age of Reason* was unpopular in America, and Paine became a forgotten revolutionary hero for many years.

GLOSSARY

apprentice Someone who works for a skilled person in order to learn a trade or profession.

aristocrat A member of the ruling class or of the nobility.

Boston Tea Party An important event when a group of colonists, known as the Sons of Liberty, stood up against unfair British taxes. They boarded ships and threw the tea into the Boston Harbor.

corset A close-fitting undergarment, worn by women, that supports and shapes the waistline and hips.

democracy Government by the people or their elected representatives.

elite A group of people who enjoy superior social, intellectual, or economic status.

militia A group of citizens who are part of the military service.

patriot A person who supports and defends their country.

sedition Speech or behavior that is directed against the peace of a state.

strife Angry or violent struggle or conflict.

tyranny A government that uses terrible force to control the people.

INDEX